THIS JOURNAL BELONGS TO

....

Copyright © 2022 by Hay House, Inc.

Published in the United States by:
Hay House, Inc.: www.hayhouse.com®

Published in Australia by:
Hay House Australia Pty. Ltd.: www.hayhouse.com.au

Published in the United Kingdom by:
Hay House UK, Ltd.: www.hayhouse.co.uk

Published in India by:
Hay House Publishers India: www.hayhouse.co.in

Cover & Interior Design: Ashley Prine, Tandem Books
Cover Illustration: © Suzanne Washington
Image Credits: Shutterstock: Back cover & interior decorative elements used
throughout © LeKodesign; 6, 18, 32, 44, 68, 90, 98, 120 (mandala corners)
© Marina Demidova, (glowing star pattern) © Tanya Antusenok, (background
texture) © Apostrophe; 9 © Katika; 21, 35, 123 © sliplee; 28, 29, 58, 59, 80,
81, 96, 97, 110, 111 (pattern) © anvinoart; 80 (chakras) © Tata.Ya; 81 (lotus)
© Litanut; 97 (torso) © kichikimi; 97 (hand) © Viktoriia_M; 101 © TAMSAM;
110 (crystals) © Benny Koha; 111 © Greazel

The author of this book does not dispense medical advice or prescribe the use
of any technique as a form of treatment for physical, emotional, or medical
problems without the advice of a physician, either directly or indirectly. The
intent of the author is only to offer information of a general nature to help you
in your quest for emotional, physical, and spiritual well-being. In the event
you use any of the information in this book for yourself, the author and the
publisher assume no responsibility for your actions.

Tradepaper ISBN: 978-1-4019-7243-1

10 9 8 7 6 5 4 3 2 1

1st edition, November 2022

Printed in the United States of America

POSITIVE MANIFESTATION

Journal

INSPIRATIONAL PROMPTS & EXERCISES
FOR CREATING THE LIFE OF YOUR DREAMS

The Hay House Editors

HAY HOUSE, INC.
Carlsbad, California • New York City
London • Sydney • New Delhi

INTRODUCTION

YOUR POWER, YOUR PATH

Hello, and welcome to your journal journey into manifesting the life of your dreams! In these pages, you'll discover your inner power and how to put it into action to create the reality you want. That's what manifestation is all about—uncovering the power within yourself, which is one and the same with the power of all creation. The whole universe is vibrating with energy, and you're part of it. It's easy to lose sight of this connection, though, and when you do, you're left feeling out of sync and without control. But the truth is you are one with the great universal energy field, sending out and receiving vibrations, much like a satellite. And like a satellite, what you send out and receive depends on your programming, the frequency you're tuned to. You do this regardless of whether or not you're aware of it, but when you become aware of it, you begin to realize and channel your power to manifest your reality.

This all comes down to the Law of Attraction: you draw to yourself the vibrations you put out. If you put out negativity, fear, and pessimism, you'll attract those things. If you put out positivity, love, and peace, then that's what you'll attract. Of course it's easier said than done to shift your energy from negative to positive. While the work is uplifting and often enjoyable, it still takes commitment and effort, and that's where this journal comes in.

Throughout these pages, you'll explore different concepts and exercises for sending out and attracting positive energy so you can manifest your desires. You'll learn how to tap into the universal energy field, raise your vibration, set your intentions, recognize signs from the universe, and clear away blockages in your flow so you can manifest love, abundance, and peace, and much more. Some of these practices will strongly resonate with you, and you'll find yourself pursuing them in more depth, while others won't speak to you. And that's perfectly fine. If they don't serve you, let them go.

Because while we are all part of one creation, we are also individuals, and our paths to connecting with the universal energy field are all different. Some people see manifestation through a scientific lens, while others see it spiritually. Whether you see synchronous signs as messages from the Divine, perhaps from angels, or as indications that your energy is vibrating at the optimal frequency, you're right. All of these viewpoints are equally effective and real, because as you'll soon explore, your thoughts create your reality, and that's your greatest power. There is no right or wrong path, only your own path. You manifest your world through what you think and do, and as long as you follow your own path, one that is truly and authentically yours, that's the truth. That's your power.

Getting on that path takes care and time, because to truly be yourself, you have to clear away baggage you've picked up throughout your life. Figuring out what is your truth and what is a belief imposed on you takes careful inspection, because we've been hearing what other people think since the time we're born. You'll discover that some things that feel like truths are actually limiting beliefs—blocks you can knock out of your way. Once you clear these things away, you will feel the joy and comfort of following your very own path. You will begin to vibrate in beautiful harmony with the universe as you manifest your dreams.

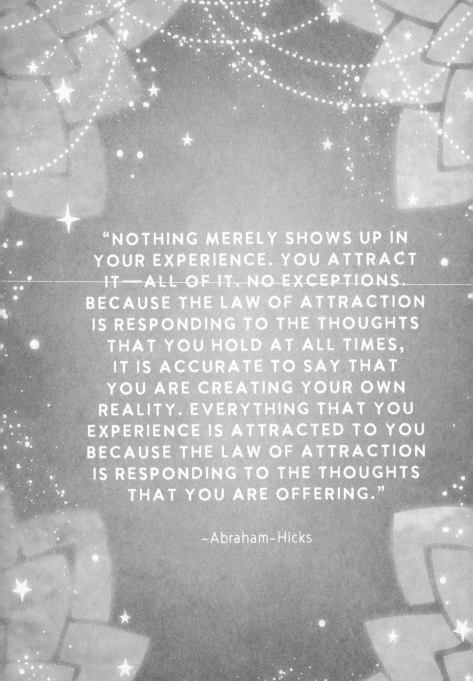

"NOTHING MERELY SHOWS UP IN YOUR EXPERIENCE. YOU ATTRACT IT—ALL OF IT. NO EXCEPTIONS. BECAUSE THE LAW OF ATTRACTION IS RESPONDING TO THE THOUGHTS THAT YOU HOLD AT ALL TIMES, IT IS ACCURATE TO SAY THAT YOU ARE CREATING YOUR OWN REALITY. EVERYTHING THAT YOU EXPERIENCE IS ATTRACTED TO YOU BECAUSE THE LAW OF ATTRACTION IS RESPONDING TO THE THOUGHTS THAT YOU ARE OFFERING."

–Abraham-Hicks

REMEMBERING THE LAW
OF ATTRACTION

The Law of Attraction—the belief that you get back whatever you put out—is foundational to manifesting the reality you want. Truly understanding this law is sometimes described as an act of remembering rather than learning. This is because deep down you know the truth of what you desire, but that truth can be forgotten or obscured by other ideas. One way to allow the truth of the Law of Attraction to fully emerge in your mind is to think back to when you've already experienced it yourself, as we all have throughout our lives.

Recall and write about a time when you thought of something—whether it was positive or negative—that you wanted or wanted to avoid and then saw those thoughts manifest in your reality.

continued . . .

YOU ARE IT

We are able to manifest our reality through thoughts because our thoughts *are* that reality. You, your body, the world around you, this journal are all dense patterns of energy. Even though matter feels solid, the fundamental particles that make it up are themselves amazingly tiny and dense bits of energy. Our thoughts are able to interact directly with physical reality because they are all part of the same energy field.

It can be difficult to fully accept the energetic reality of the world, especially of your own body, because conventional wisdom and your senses tend to tell you otherwise. But as you've surely experienced before, things are not always as they first seem. Write about a time in your life when you discovered that something you took for granted was not what you first thought it was.

....

....

....

....

....

....

You can begin to get in touch with the energetic reality of your being by observing it. Sit facing a white wall. Hold your hands in front of you, a couple inches apart, palms facing each other. Relax your eyes and concentrate on feeling the energy of your being for a few minutes. What did you see?

ALL OF IT

The feeling of separateness is another idea we get from conventional wisdom and our senses. You look around and see that you are separate from the things around you, from the other people in the world, but the truth is that everything is part of the same energetic field. We are all one in a very real and meaningful way.

Absorbing that truth and realizing what it is that allows you to feel tuned in and out will help you attract and manifest what you want. Here, reflect on the idea of oneness. When do you most feel at one with creation? What makes you feel separate?

....

....

....

....

....

....

....

SYNCING IN

When you experience a coincidence—that is, two seemingly unrelated things that happen without a conventionally obvious connection but nonetheless feel meaningfully connected—that's a synchronicity. Maybe you come across a picture of an old friend you haven't talked to in a while and then they call you the next day, or you stop at the store to pick something up and the total comes to $11.11 and it's 11:11 in the morning.

People tend to dismiss these types of events as funny flukes, but synchronicities feel meaningful because they are meaningful. They can bring you closer to something you want or somewhere you'd like to go. Synchronicities are signs that you're on the right path.

Write about a few synchronicities you have experienced in the past.

....

....

....

....

....

....

....

Send out the thought that you will experience a synchronicity within the next couple days, then keep your eyes and mind open for it. What did you experience? Where did it lead you or your thoughts? (If you don't have this journal with you when you experience it, you can note it on your phone or jot it down on whatever you have near you so you can reflect on it here later.)

RECOGNIZE YOUR INNER POWER

*I*t can take a little while for the idea that your thoughts can manifest reality to really sink in. Even when you believe it's true, sometimes you need to see it in action before you really *feel* it's true.

To start feeling the truth of your own power, decide you're going to get some good news sometime in the next day or so. Write below how you expect good news with complete assurance, then keep an eye out for it.

What good news did you get?

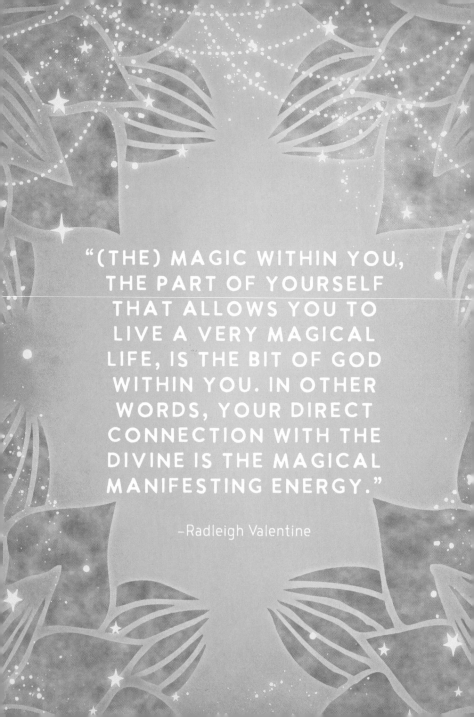

"(THE) MAGIC WITHIN YOU, THE PART OF YOURSELF THAT ALLOWS YOU TO LIVE A VERY MAGICAL LIFE, IS THE BIT OF GOD WITHIN YOU. IN OTHER WORDS, YOUR DIRECT CONNECTION WITH THE DIVINE IS THE MAGICAL MANIFESTING ENERGY."

–Radleigh Valentine

MANY NAMES, ONE SOURCE

There are many descriptions out there for the energy of life and creation that surrounds us and that we are connected to and also composed of. Some call it spiritual, magical, divine, or even God, while others tend toward more scientific and physical explanations. When it comes to harmonizing with this energy so that you can consciously manifest your deepest dreams and desires, what matters is the personal connection you feel with this great source of power.

How would you describe the source? How does your connection to it feel?

....

....

....

....

....

....

....

....

continued . . .

ZEN OUT COLORING

GRATEFUL VIBES

Since everything is made of energetic vibrations, it's important that your own energy has good vibes, so to speak. By raising your energetic vibration, you can better attract what you want from the universe, and it feels good to boot! One of the best ways to raise your vibration is through practicing gratitude.

On these pages, reflect on what you're grateful for in your life. You can go big, small, and everything in between.

....

....

....

....

....

....

....

....

....

FEEL THE MOMENT

When you are present in the moment, you raise your vibration and ability to attract good. The past and future are imaginary, while the present is the truth, and being mindful of the moment helps you see your path. This exercise will help you get in touch with the present, and you can call back on it anytime you're feeling disconnected from the moment.

Take some deep breaths and become aware of what's around you. Try to notice subtle sounds and smells and other sensory input you might not always recognize. Feel yourself in the present and your connection to your surroundings.

Write down everything you noticed.

....

....

....

....

....

....

....

THE NATURAL WAY

Spending time outdoors is a wonderful way to raise your vibration. By getting out into nature, you get some exercise through walking or hiking, take a break from energy-draining screens, and get some lovely vitamin D from the sun—and that's just to start. Connecting with Mother Nature realigns your energy with Hers. The feel of the breeze, the sound of it in the leaves, the feeling of the sun on your skin, the whole experience elevates you, putting you in sync with the wonders of the natural world.

Go to one of your favorite outdoor spots and soak in all that positive, growing energy, then sketch the scene around you here.

THE POWER OF INTENTION

Within the field of energy that makes up the universe is the power of intention, which is also called the force of intention, because it is indeed a force. It is everywhere, all around you, active in all things. You can see it in how the seed of a tree holds everything that that tree will become—the bark, the leaves, its flowers, and the seeds it will create. You can see it in yourself in the beating of your heart, the color of your eyes, and all the things that you think and do. It is the infinite potential of all things, both physical and nonphysical.

Dr. Wayne W. Dyer in his book *The Power of Intention* says we have become disconnected from intention because of our egos, the ideas we have of ourselves that revolve around the things we have and do, what people think of us, and how we feel separate from other people and the universe. But you can reconnect to the power of intention by letting go of those ego ideas. Once you do, you will be on your path to attracting all manner of good to you.

Dr. Dyer says there are four stages to letting go of ego and tapping into the power of intention:

1. Disciplining your body with healthy foods, exercise, and good habits that are driven not by ego but by the natural self.

2. Developing the wisdom to focus and be patient with yourself as your thoughts realign.

3. Loving what you do, doing what you love.

4. Surrendering to the force of intention in the universe and allowing yourself to be carried by it.

Once you've surrendered to intention, you are in touch with your true soul and have the power to go wherever you are destined to go. You are no longer caught up in the trappings of ego.

Take some time to reflect on the power of intention. Where do you think your path would take you if you were able to let go of your ego?

BODY WORSHIP

*C*onnecting to the power of intention means letting go of your ego, but that doesn't mean neglecting your body. To come into harmony with the energy of the universe, you have to be in harmony with physical being. This means forming a positive relationship with your body and discovering what to eat, how to move, and what kinds of self-care work best for you. This may seem like work on the surface, but it's actually acts of worshipping your body like the sacred temple it is.

What is your relationship with your body like?

....

....

....

....

....

....

....

....

*What acts of worshipping your body would you like to
make routine?*

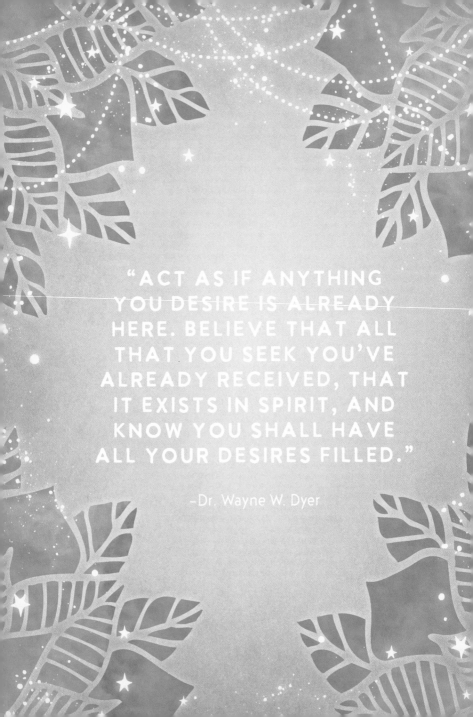

"ACT AS IF ANYTHING YOU DESIRE IS ALREADY HERE. BELIEVE THAT ALL THAT YOU SEEK YOU'VE ALREADY RECEIVED, THAT IT EXISTS IN SPIRIT, AND KNOW YOU SHALL HAVE ALL YOUR DESIRES FILLED."

–Dr. Wayne W. Dyer

WHAT DO YOU DESIRE?

Tapping into the power of intention and being able to manifest what you desire is not about trying to bend the energy of the universe to your will. It's about riding the wave instead of trying to fight through it. It's about coming into harmony with the power of intention so you can recognize and receive the blessings that already surround you on your path.

What is it that you most desire, deep down?

....

....

....

....

....

....

....

....

....

continued . . .

Concentrate on those desires as you color this page to build up that vibration.

WHAT YOU *DON'T* DESIRE

$\mathcal{C}$oming into harmony with the source energy of the universe so you can manifest your deep desires is not only about knowing what you really want but also about knowing what you *don't* want. You attract both good and bad things to you with your thoughts, so you need to be clear about what you do and don't want. For instance, if you want to attract confidence, you can focus on intentionally putting that signal out there, instead of putting out the signal of, say, fear and unintentionally attracting that.

What don't you desire?

....

....

....

....

....

....

....

....

....

What signals have you been putting out lately? Reflect on how they align with what you desire and what you don't desire.

SET YOUR INTENTION

*N*ow that you've learned about the natural power of intention and thought deeply about what you desire and what you don't, you can set a specific intention that you want to manifest. What do you want your days to look like? How do you want to feel in that relationship? What do you want to bring into your life that will help you feel fulfilled?

Reflect on what you wrote in the last two entries, then write your intention below with as much clarity and detail as you can.

....

....

....

....

....

....

....

....

Come back to this page and write down a simplified version of your intention several times a day for as many days as it takes to fill the page. This will reinforce your intention and keep your energy on track.

....

....

....

....

....

....

....

....

....

....

....

....

FEEL THE TRUTH

*B*elieving your intention will come to pass can be tricky when you first start out on your path to manifestation. Believing deep down that you deserve the life of your dreams and will get what you desire takes a lot of courage, and usually people have to undo a lot of negative thought habits and pessimism.

You can work toward positive beliefs by imagining that you already have what you desire. Write as if your intention has already manifested. How does it feel?

....

....

....

....

....

....

....

....

TAKE AUTHENTIC ACTION

A major part of manifesting your desires is working in collaboration with the universe by taking heartfelt steps toward your intention. You are co-creating your desires, which means you have to work toward your goals with real action. For instance, if you want to perfect an art, you need to practice it.

What actions will you take to manifest your intention? Be as detailed as possible with your plan.

....

....

....

....

....

....

....

....

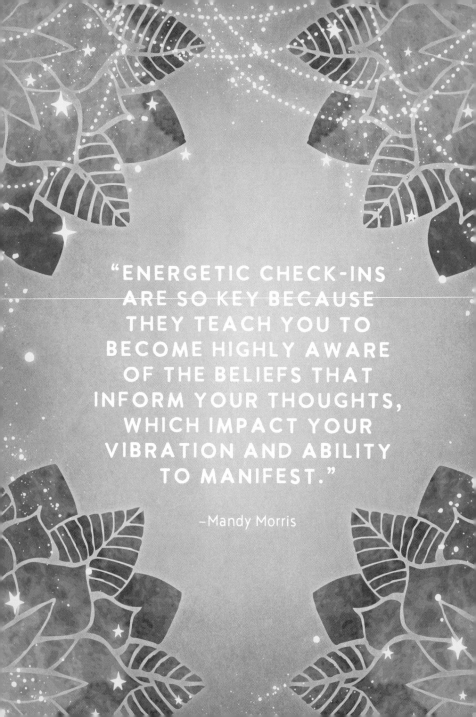

"ENERGETIC CHECK-INS
ARE SO KEY BECAUSE
THEY TEACH YOU TO
BECOME HIGHLY AWARE
OF THE BELIEFS THAT
INFORM YOUR THOUGHTS,
WHICH IMPACT YOUR
VIBRATION AND ABILITY
TO MANIFEST."

–Mandy Morris

REGULAR CHECK-INS

*C*hecking in with yourself regularly allows you to become aware of the energy you're emitting throughout the day. Once you're aware of what you're signaling and mindful of being in the present, you can raise your vibration when needed so you can keep on the path of manifesting your intention.

How are you feeling right now? Why do you feel that way? Are you in the moment or focused on the past or future?

continued . . .

Now set alarms to go off twice more later today, and when they go off, come back and answer those questions again. Mentally repeat these check-ins every day, and soon it will be a valuable habit.

1st Check-in: How are you feeling right now? Why do you feel that way? Are you in the moment or focused on the past or future?

....

....

....

....

....

....

....

....

....

....

2nd Check-in: How are you feeling right now? Why do you feel that way? Are you in the moment or focused on the past or future?

....

....

....

....

....

....

....

....

....

....

....

....

RELEASING NEGATIVE ENERGY

When you start to check in with your feelings regularly, you'll notice that you have some habitual thoughts, feelings, and reactions that you've picked up in your life but that don't serve you. These negativities are usually rooted in a bad experience from the past that you're afraid will repeat in the future, and they take you off the path of manifesting your true desires. Recognizing where these negative patterns come from and how they hold you back will help you shift your mindset so you can release them.

What is a negative habitual feeling or thought that comes up for you?

....

....

....

....

....

....

....

Where did it come from, and how did it help you then? How is it holding you back now?

....

....

....

....

....

What is a more positive way of framing the same feeling or thought?

....

....

....

....

....

....

IT'S ALL AN AFFIRMATION

We usually think of affirmations as positive statements said with intention, and while they are that, everything you think and say, positive or negative, is also an affirmation. If you say negative things, you affirm negative outcomes, while speaking positively will affirm positive outcomes. As Louise Hay put it, if you plant a tomato seed, only a tomato plant can grow from it.

You can counter negative speech by having a positive affirmation at the ready to say instead. What are some negative things you find yourself saying regularly? This includes deflecting compliments or belittling your achievements or efforts!

....

....

....

....

....

....

....

Rewrite those negative sentiments into positive affirmations you will say instead from now on.

....

....

....

....

....

....

....

....

....

....

....

....

SEND AND RECEIVE LOVE

You can manifest so much good in your life using the Law of Attraction, including love of all types. Since we get what we put out, the best thing you can do to draw love to you is to send love out. Meditate for a few minutes on the feeling of love, thinking about the people whom you love.

Write down the names of all the people you love and something great about them.

....

....

....

....

....

....

....

....

....

....

....

....

....

....

....

....

Now write about a person you want to be in a loving relationship with, whether it's a romantic partner you don't yet know or a person in your life with whom you want to foster love. Be as specific as you can about that person and the feeling of love you want with them.

ALLOW ABUNDANCE IN

Think of something you want lots and lots of in your life. It can be friends, success, wealth, health, or whatever you've always wanted but thought you couldn't have. Meditate for a few minutes on the idea that abundance is all around you. There is plenty for everyone, including you. You can access this abundance by being open to the signs the universe is giving you that point you down the path to abundance.

What negative thoughts come up when you think of abundance? What mental blocks do you have that make you feel like you can't actually have what you want in abundance?

....

....

....

....

....

....

....

Now draw a symbol (or a few symbols) of those mental blocks. Then cross them out. Really obliterate them. Focus on knocking them down and leaving them behind.

PEACE BE WITH YOU

*L*ife can be hectic and demand so much from you that it's easy to slip into a go-go-go mentality, and what goes-goes-goes away with that can be a sense of centeredness and inner peace. When you're caught up in that energy, you end up feeling drained and can slip off your path and into negative patterns. To manifest peace, sit for a few minutes and meditate on your breath, on just feeling peaceful. Then imagine yourself as a satellite transmitting that peace to the people you know, to your town, to the world. By giving off the positive energy you desire, you will attract it to you.

Write about your experience with this meditation. What thoughts came up that made you feel most peaceful?

....

....

....

....

....

....

....

DREAM INCUBATION

Your dreams can be powerful conduits for finding answers to questions, uncovering deep truths about the self, or manifesting creativity, confidence, and desired outcomes through a practice called dream incubation. By focusing on a question or desire before you go to sleep, you can prompt your subconscious mind to release an answer that's been brewing deep in your thoughts but that you have yet to articulate. You may also be able to tap into the universal energy to attract an outcome you're hoping for.

Your dreams will then answer you, most likely using symbols. When you wake in the morning or from a dream, you need to immediately write anything you remember about your dreams. Don't worry about writing logically or even in sentences. Just quickly write whatever you remember. After you have everything down, reflect on what you wrote. There are many resources you can use for checking out what different symbols might mean, but your dreams and their language are your own. Most likely they mean whatever *you* think they mean.

Tonight, before you go to bed, write down a question you have, maybe about how to move forward in some part of your life or what your deeper purpose is.

....

....

....

....

What did you dream last night? As you reflect on your dreams, do you see a potential answer to your question? Remember, dreams often speak in symbols and feelings, not in clear sentences and phrases.

....

....

....

....

....

....

....

....

....

....

....

....

DREAM SIGNS

*D*reams, whether you incubate them or not, provide windows into the deepest part of your mind and even connect to the universal energy all around you. They can give you guidance about your path to manifesting your desires if you keep an eye out for the signs and keep your mind open to interpreting them. For instance, a dream about finding some cash in your pocket probably isn't literally telling you to check your pockets, but it could be showing you that there will be an opportunity to increase your wealth coming up, so stay open. Or if you see a butterfly in a dream and then also in waking life, that butterfly is a message for you that you need to interpret by trusting your instincts.

What are some of your recurring dreams or dream symbols?

....

....

....

....

....

....

....

What do you think they mean?

FOLLOW YOUR DREAMS

When you are tuned in to the energy of the universe, it can pay off to literally follow your dreams. If you find yourself in a particular place in a dream, talking to someone you know, or doing something you can otherwise do in your waking life, follow those signs and actually go to that place, talk to that person, do that thing. It might just lead you down your path to somewhere you want to be!

What things have you dreamed about recently that you could do in your waking life? Try to remember as much detail as you can.

....

....

....

....

....

....

....

....

Follow those dream signs in your waking life, then write about the experience. Where did the signs take you?

EVERYWHERE ARE SIGNS

The waking world is also full of signs if you look for them. Once you put out the desire to see signs, they will appear! Synchronicities are the most important ones to look out for, like when you see the same number over and over again in a day, or you want to manifest wealth and keep finding pennies, or you experience anything that makes you think, *What a weird coincidence!*

Today, practice being on the careful lookout for signs. Notice everything you can, and don't dismiss anything that catches your eye. Write down every potential sign you see.

Reflect on the signs you saw and write about what you think they may mean. Remember to trust your instincts.

TRUST YOURSELF

To become more in tune with the signs from the universe, it's important to trust yourself. You are like a satellite sending and receiving messages, and the more you trust yourself, the more powerfully you'll be able to send and receive. This means that anytime your senses tingle even a little bit, you're receiving a sign, so pay attention. If something in you is saying "yes" or "no," listen. The signs and messages may be subtle at first, but the more you learn to be open to them, the easier they will be to see.

What is something small that's happened recently that tugged at you as important but you dismissed it?

To build trust in yourself, ask the universe for a sign and then look out for it over the next day. Keep your eyes and mind open and allow your intuition to guide you.

What sign did you receive and how did that experience feel?

....

....

....

....

....

....

....

....

....

....

"WHEN I'M MISALIGNED,
I TRY TO CONTROL MY
CIRCUMSTANCES. . . . WHEN
I,M IN ALIGNMENT WITH THE
UNIVERSE, I FEEL HAPPY AND
EXCITED REGARDLESS OF
WHAT MY CIRCUMSTANCES
MAY BE. . . GOOD THINGS
FLOW TO ME, AND I FEEL
CREATIVITY MOVING
THROUGH ME. PEOPLE WANT
TO SUPPORT ME, AND I FIND
A WAY THROUGH
EVERY BLOCK."

–Gabrielle Bernstein

BREAKING BLOCKS

*B*eing in positive flow with the universe is so important for manifesting your desires. When you face each day knowing you're going to get what you need to follow your path and be supported, good things happen. Fears you've developed over your life, though, can act as blocks in that flow, cutting you off from attracting what you want, especially when you focus really hard on trying to control things instead of trusting that the universe has you.

When kind of situations do you most try to control? What fear is at the root of that?

....

....

....

....

....

....

....

continued . . .

Now, write a letter forgiving yourself for that fear.

Finally, think of the best feeling you could have right now and quickly write about it. Whatever comes up first is where the universe is guiding you, so trust that whatever it is is the next step you need.

LET IT GO

*I*t takes work to let go of long-held negative beliefs you have about yourself, but it's the best kind of work. It breaks up energy blocks, empowers you to attract positivity, and allows you to feel happier with yourself and more peaceful about your path.

For instance, if you say negative things to yourself about your body, you know that brings your energy low. Imagine if instead you told yourself how well your body serves you, how your legs take you where you want to go, how your arms carry what you need. What would your energy be like then?

What negative ideas do you have about yourself? Skip a line between each one. Then, go back, cross out each negative idea, and write a positive affirmation about yourself. For instance, if you have a negative body image, write about all the wonderful things your body does for you.

....

....

....

....

....

....

EXCUSE YOU

*I*t's a common thing for people to come up with reasons why they can't have something they really want. They create excuses for not going after their dreams, but those excuses are really just cover-ups for a deeply held fear that makes them believe they don't actually deserve to get what they want. Unmasking those excuses will go a long way to replacing your fears with trust in your path through the universe.

What are some excuses you make for not going after something you really want?

....

....

....

....

....

....

....

....

What fears are those excuses masking?

I SEE YOU, FEAR

ear is something we all learn over the course of our lives to help us feel safe and in control when we might be in danger, but fear can also act like a trap, walling us inside a story about what we can't do and can't have and knocking us off our path to manifesting our dreams. The first step to banishing fear is recognizing fear when it happens. This may sound easy, but fear is tricky. It wears many masks—laziness, insecurity, making excuses, perfectionism, anger, pride, the need to please. These negative emotions and many others prevent you from doing something, from reaching out, from being positive and receptive.

Think of a story that you tell yourself that has held you back. Write about it in detail and try to see where the fear is in the story and where it comes from.

....

....

....

....

....

....

DISARMING FEAR

Really understanding the basis of your fear and then sending yourself love and compassion in place of it is how you disarm fear.

Think about a time recently when you felt fear, or another negative emotion that was really based in fear, and it made you react negatively. Write about it in detail, and as you do, notice what emotions you have and any sensations that come up in your body.

....

....

....

....

....

....

....

....

Once you are immersed in the feelings of the experience, hug yourself and send yourself love and compassion to places where you feel emotions and sensations. Continue to hug yourself and send love to yourself as the emotions run their course, and don't stop until they lose their sharpness.

Afterward, come up with some affirmations you can use to call up that feeling of love conquering fear.

CLEARING YOUR CHAKRAS

The chakras are energy centers in your body. While some systems name as many as 78,000 chakras throughout the body, there are 7 major ones:

 The **crown chakra** is associated with your spirituality and the universe.

 The **third-eye chakra** is linked to intuition, imagination, and psychic abilities.

 The **throat chakra relates** to communication, creativity, and your truth.

 The **heart chakra** is filled with compassion and love.

 The **solar plexus chakra** is concerned with willpower and intellect.

 The **sacral chakra** is connected to emotions, sexuality, and creation.

 The **root chakra** (aka the base chakra) connects to the earth and embodies the survival instinct.

When your chakras are spinning freely, you are vibrating in harmony with the universe. When one or more chakras are blocked, spinning counterclockwise, or overactive, your whole system can get thrown off, leaving you sluggish, overwhelmed, and feeling cut off from the universal flow.

To identify a blocked chakra, try the Clear Your Chakras exercise on the next page. See if you can sense how your chakras are spinning and whether you're holding tension in any of them. Trust your intuition.

CLEAR YOUR CHAKRAS

If you feel a blocked chakra or just want to raise your vibration, you can do so with a simple meditation. Lie down in a comfortable position and breathe deeply. Hover your hand over your base chakra and imagine it spinning freely, sending energy throughout your body. Then move up through the chakras, imagining them each in turn spinning freely. If you sense any blockages, spend extra time with that chakra.

What thoughts and feelings came up for you as you did this exercise?

....

....

....

....

....

....

....

....

MANIFESTING THROUGH YOUR CHAKRAS

*V*isualizing what you want to manifest through your chakras is a powerful tool to help you stay open and in flow with the universe. Go through the following steps and write about your experience with each one. Be on the lookout for insights and clarity.

Crown chakra: *This is where inspiration and energy enter your mind. Think of something you intend to manifest and imagine it coming into you through this chakra from the universe.*

....

....

Third-eye chakra: *Intuition lives here. Picture your intention in this third eye and intuit what you need to do to realize it, as well as any blocks you might have.*

....

....

Throat chakra: *Bring your intention to this chakra and speak it out loud. Think of people you could communicate your intention to who might be able to help you achieve it.*

....

....

Heart chakra: *Allow your intention to rest in your heart where you feel love for it and yourself.*

....

....

Solar plexus chakra: *Move your intention to this chakra and feel your willpower, your courage, and your intellect vibrating around it and through it, giving you the strength you need to overcome any obstacle.*

....

....

Sacral chakra: *Send your intention to this chakra to become energized with the passion that burns inside you.*

....

....

Root chakra: *As your intention settles into your root chakra, it connects to the earth, to the physical world where you manifest it into your reality.*

....

....

HOW'S IT GOING?

Now that you've been working on connecting with the universal energy and clearing any blocks you might have on your path to manifesting your desires, check in with yourself and your energy.

How have you been feeling lately? Are you usually in the moment, or are you more focused on the past or the future?

....

....

....

....

....

....

....

....

....

....

When do you feel most in tune with the universal energy?

....

....

....

....

....

What have you manifested for yourself?

....

....

....

....

....

....

RECOGNIZING YOUR
PERSONAL CHALLENGES

Tuning in to the energy of the universe is an ongoing process. While it certainly gets easier over time when you consistently work on it, we all have specific challenges, unique to our own experiences, that can throw us off. Hurtful or even traumatic events in your past leave deep impressions, and when something reminds you of that past hurt, it can put you off your path and lead you to send out negative energy that's buried deep within you. Sometimes a trigger is very obvious—seeing a person who hurt you, perhaps—or it can be subtler, like a song or smell that sets something off in your subconscious. The best thing you can do to keep in control is to learn to recognize these causes quickly so you can work on managing them.

What are some things that you find personally challenging? Try to write as freely as you can. If something comes to mind, don't analyze whether or not it's really triggering; just write it down.

....

....

....

....

....

What do those triggers feel like in your body? Once you become aware of the feelings they cause, you can recognize them and deal with them more quickly.

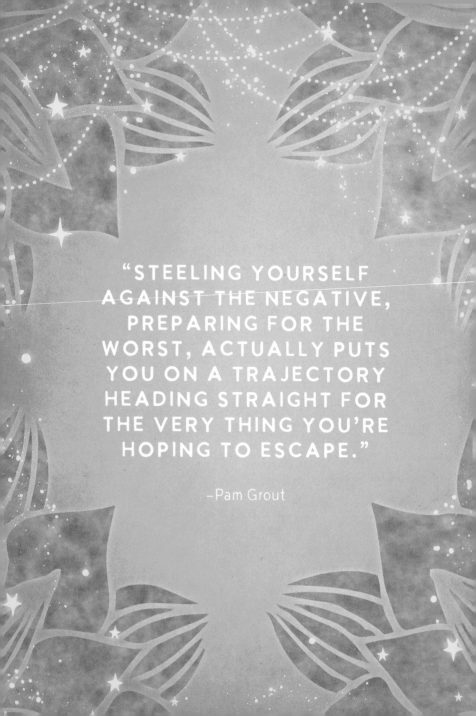

"STEELING YOURSELF AGAINST THE NEGATIVE, PREPARING FOR THE WORST, ACTUALLY PUTS YOU ON A TRAJECTORY HEADING STRAIGHT FOR THE VERY THING YOU'RE HOPING TO ESCAPE."

–Pam Grout

UNRAVELING YOUR TRIGGERS

When you put a lot of thought and energy into fearing something and trying to avoid it, as we often do with the things that trigger us, we sometimes attract that very thing we want to avoid. Now that you have brought a conscious awareness to your personal challenges and the feelings that come up with them, you can work on getting to the bottom of them so you can ultimately spend less time with those thoughts and feelings. You can do this through tapping, which you will explore soon, and by putting the thoughts that come from your triggers on trial with a series of questions that help you better understand your emotions and release whatever pain you're holding surrounding it. The next time you feel triggered, ask yourself the following questions, and write down short, honest answers.

What caused you to feel this way?

....

....

....

....

....

....

continued . . .

What are you feeling and where in your body are you feeling it?

....

....

....

....

....

What outcome are you afraid is going to happen?

....

....

....

....

....

....

What is the best-possible outcome you can think of happening?

....

....

....

....

....

Now take some deep breaths and focus on the best-possible outcome. How does thinking about this make you feel and where in your body do you feel it?

....

....

....

....

....

DO INTERRUPT

When you're feeling triggered, or you've had any kind of negative experience, or you're just feeling low energy and want a boost, you can retune your energy and increase your vibration using what manifestation and authentic-living expert Mandy Morris calls "pattern interrupts." These shift your thoughts and therefore your energy, nudging you out of the negative and into the positive. They can be almost anything you like, the key word here being *like*. They can be physical, like doing some quick jumping jacks or dancing to a favorite song. They can be mental, like taking 10 meditative breaths or writing down what's bothering you. Or they can be spiritual, like saying a prayer or visualizing opening up your chakras.

Try some of these pattern interrupts or come up with your own, and write about which ones work best for you.

....

....

....

....

....

....

TAP INTO YOUR ENERGY

Tapping, also known as emotional freedom technique (EFT), is a simple practice that clears blockages to rebalance the energy in your body and help you overcome limiting beliefs and heal from your triggers. It is also a great tool for raising your vibration. It's like a very gentle form of self-acupressure. To start, identify a block you'd like to clear, your "most pressing issue." Let's say you want to decrease your anxiety.

Sum up the issue you'd like to work on, then express that you love and accept yourself, despite the issue. This is your "setup statement." For example: "Even though I feel anxious and overwhelmed, I deeply love and accept myself." Then come up with a shortened form of your setup statement: your "reminder phrase." With our example, you might say "This anxiety . . ." or "I'm anxious and overwhelmed . . ."

....

....

Next, take one or two fingers and tap on the side of your hand while saying your setup statement three times. Then assess how you feel.

....

....

....

The tapping points illustration shows the eight points you'll be tapping on in sequence: eyebrow, side of eye, under eye, under nose, chin, collarbone, under arm, then top of head. Tap on each point several times, saying your reminder phrase out loud, before moving on to the next point.

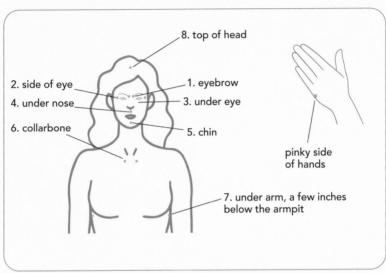

8. top of head

2. side of eye

4. under nose

6. collarbone

1. eyebrow

3. under eye

5. chin

pinky side of hands

7. under arm, a few inches below the armpit

Once you've completed a cycle, assess how you feel. How does it compare to what you wrote earlier?

....

....

....

Continue tapping on the eight points in the sequence, if needed, until you feel the blocks around the issue beginning to clear.

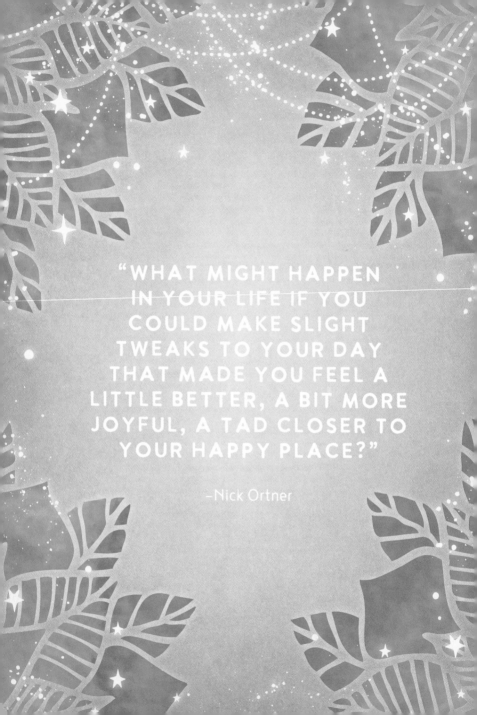

"WHAT MIGHT HAPPEN IN YOUR LIFE IF YOU COULD MAKE SLIGHT TWEAKS TO YOUR DAY THAT MADE YOU FEEL A LITTLE BETTER, A BIT MORE JOYFUL, A TAD CLOSER TO YOUR HAPPY PLACE?"

–Nick Ortner

TAP INTO HAPPINESS

Nick Ortner, EFT expert and CEO of The Tapping Solution, pairs his tapping practice with important acts of self-care in order to manifest his best self and his best life. By prioritizing moments of joy in your day, you create more happiness for yourself and raise your vibration—and making tapping part of that can give you an even bigger boost.

Write a list of little things that make you happy, like brewing a cup of tea and chatting with friends, going for a hike, or anything that brings you joy!

....

....

....

....

....

....

....

....

continued . . .

The next time you feel your energy dipping, go through the following tapping sequence (see pages 96 and 97 for more instructions). Then pick an item from the list you write and do it!

Eyebrow: I can shift my energy.
Side of Eye: I can let myself feel good.
Under Eye: I can let myself enjoy this thing I love.
Under Nose: I can feel good while I do it.
Chin: Feeling good is safe.
Collarbone: Feelings are always changing.
Under Arm: But it's safe and good to enjoy the moment.
Top of Head: I can let myself feel good.

How do you feel now compared to before you tried this exercise?

....

....

....

....

....

....

....

....

TAP INTO GREATER ENERGY

*Y*ou can use tapping as a quick and easy way to tune your energetic vibrations. If you're feeling a little out of sync, or even if you're feeling great and want to send that out into the universe, going through a tapping sequence with a message tailored to the moment can put you right where you need to be.

How are you feeling right now? How do you want to feel?

....

....

....

....

....

....

....

....

Reflect on what you wrote and turn your answers into short statements below to use in your tapping sequence.

Eyebrow:

Side of Eye:

Under Eye:

Under Nose:

Chin:

Collarbone:

Under Arm:

Top of Head:

How do you feel now compared to before you tapped?

....

....

....

....

....

SEE YOUR POWER

A wonderful way to raise your vibration is through mirror work. By looking yourself in the eyes in the mirror and repeating affirmations, you recognize, channel, and amplify your inner power for manifestation. This is so powerful because it runs counter to what many of us do when we look in the mirror, which is to focus on what we think are our flaws and, in turn, to drag our energy down.

Mirror work can also show you where you have energy blocks. If you find it hard to say something to yourself, there is a resistance there that you may want to work on clearing. You can push through the resistance using mirror work or by going back to one of the block-clearing exercises you explored earlier in this journal.

Today, try raising your vibration with one of the greatest sources of power: self-love. Whenever you walk past a mirror, take a few seconds to look yourself in the eye and say to yourself, "I love you. You are deserving." Repeat this three times and then go about your business.

How did the mirror work feel? How did it affect your energy? Did you notice any blocks?

....

....

....

....

AFFIRMATION AMPLIFICATION

ffirmations that reinforce what you're looking to manifest become amplified when you use them for mirror work.

Write some affirmations about what you're looking to attract, whether it be love, abundance, creativity, self-love, peace, or all those things. Keep them short and positive, such as "I love and approve of myself," and continue refining them until you come up with one that really resonates with you. Then, whenever you pass a mirror today, repeat it to yourself while looking deeply into your eyes.

How did your mirror work feel today? How did it affect your energy? Did you notice any blocks?

....

....

....

....

....

....

....

....

....

....

....

....

YOU ARE THE MIRROR

So often, what you think of yourself is what you think of the world around you. If you look out and see negativity, it's usually a reflection of negativity you feel about your life. If you feel good, on the other hand, you see the good. Your views on the world reflect the respect you have for yourself to deal with the world and bring about the things you desire. When you have a healthy sense of self-respect, you naturally have an optimistic worldview. Again, what you put out, you attract.

Key to good self-respect is remembering that the *self* is what really matters. It's easy to allow your self-respect to get knocked up and down based on the opinions of others. But knowing your self and your path, relying on your self, and being responsible for your self is what allows you to be in control of your self-respect and therefore the energy you put out and attract.

Focus on your self by listing all the things you know about yourself to be true—the things you respect about yourself. Notice if any of these are judgments that came from other people, and put them on trial to see if you truly believe in them.

....

....

....

....

THE POWER OF CRYSTALS

Crystals, with their intriguing structures and natural beauty, are believed to possess and channel energy, and some may act as conductors and amplifiers for manifestation. The following crystals are believed to help you attract certain kinds of energy.

- Citrine attracts wealth and personal power.
- Green jade attracts money.
- Pink quartz attracts love.
- Rhodonite attracts emotional healing and love.
- Obsidian attracts energy and flow.
- Amethyst attracts calm.

When choosing a crystal, let your intuition guide you to it. Before you begin to work with it, you first must cleanse it. There are many different clearing methods, but we recommend one of the following: passing it through smoke, letting it sit on a windowsill to absorb sun and moonlight for 24 hours, or pouring fresh water over it.

CRYSTAL CLEAR

To use a crystal for manifesting and attracting your desires, you need to select one that has the kind of energy you're looking for (see page 110) and then infuse it with your intentions.

Write about what you're currently looking to manifest and then distill it down to an intention. Be as crystal clear as you can.

....

....

....

....

....

....

....

....

....

....

Now hold your crystal in your hand and think about your intention for a few moments. The crystal is now charged with your clear intention. You can carry it with you through the day and place it near your bed at night to attract that energy to you.

Draw your crystal here, attracting that which you desire.

YOU KNOW THE ANSWER

One resource people often overlook is their own inner guidance. When you are debating a decision, struggling to find a way forward, or otherwise trying to find answers, the best guidance you can get comes from trusting your intuition. It might come as a chance encounter, a sign you notice in the world, or an answer that just springs loudly into your mind. You will know it when you see or hear it; you just have to trust yourself and not get in your own way, that is, don't let the chatter of doubt that the conscious mind churns up undermine what you know deep down to be true.

What is an issue that's been troubling you lately that you'd like guidance on? Write about it in some detail.

....

....

....

....

....

....

....

Now, ask for a clear answer to come to you within the next two days. Believe you will get it, and keep your eyes and ears open. What answer did you receive?

HOW DO YOU FEEL NOW?

Now that you're coming to the end of your journal journey into manifestation, take a moment to check in with yourself, your path, and your energy.

How have you been feeling lately? How is this different from when you started your manifestation journey?

....

....

....

....

....

....

....

....

....

What have you manifested for yourself?

....

....

....

....

....

What would you still like to manifest?

....

....

....

....

....

....

WHAT'S BEST FOR YOU?

While manifestation and attraction are all about connecting to the one universal energy, there are many paths to achieving this. We all send and receive energy, but each of us still has our own unique signature, which means some practices will work better for you than others.

Take some time to go back over what you've written in this journal. Write about your experiences and what you found to be the most effective techniques for clearing blockages, attracting, and manifesting.

....

....

....

....

....

....

....

....

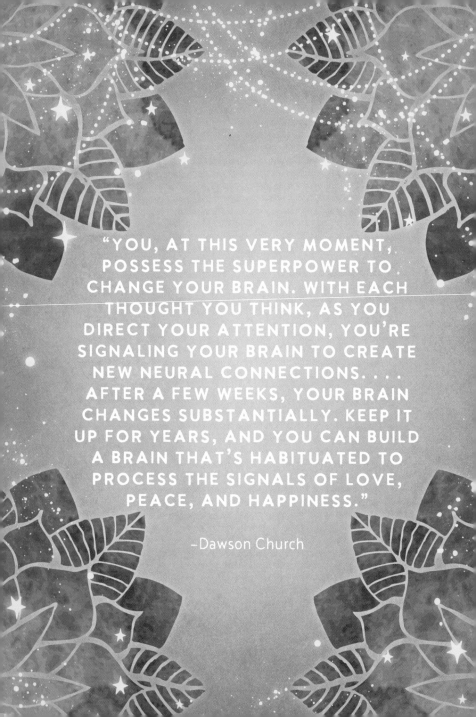

"YOU, AT THIS VERY MOMENT, POSSESS THE SUPERPOWER TO CHANGE YOUR BRAIN. WITH EACH THOUGHT YOU THINK, AS YOU DIRECT YOUR ATTENTION, YOU'RE SIGNALING YOUR BRAIN TO CREATE NEW NEURAL CONNECTIONS. . . . AFTER A FEW WEEKS, YOUR BRAIN CHANGES SUBSTANTIALLY. KEEP IT UP FOR YEARS, AND YOU CAN BUILD A BRAIN THAT'S HABITUATED TO PROCESS THE SIGNALS OF LOVE, PEACE, AND HAPPINESS."

–Dawson Church

A LIFELONG JOURNEY

Attracting and manifesting what you want for your life and for your world can be a lifelong journey that brings untold benefits not just to yourself but to those around you. And the longer you walk this path, the more powerful you become at sending out and receiving good.

What do you want to manifest for yourself in the next year, the next five years, the next ten?

....

....

....

....

....

....

....

....

....

continued . . .

What do you want to manifest for the people around you? For the whole wide world?

....

....

....

....

....

....

....

....

....

....

....

....

ZEN OUT COLORING

Hay House Titles of Related Interest

Evening Meditations Journal,
by The Hay House Editors

*The Gift of Gratitude: A Guided Journal for
Counting Your Blessings,*
by Louise Hay

The High 5 Daily Journal,
by Mel Robbins

Living Your Purpose Journal,
by Dr. Wayne W. Dyer

Morning Meditations Journal,
by The Hay House Editors

Zen Meditations Journal,
by The Hay House Editors

Sweet Dreams Journal,
by The Hay House Editors

All of the above are available at your local bookstore,
or may be ordered by contacting Hay House (see next page).

* * *

We hope you enjoyed this Hay House book. If you'd like to receive our online catalog featuring additional information on Hay House books and products, or if you'd like to find out more about the Hay Foundation, please contact:

Hay House, Inc., P.O. Box 5100, Carlsbad, CA 92018-5100
(760) 431-7695 or (800) 654-5126
(760) 431-6948 (fax) or (800) 650-5115 (fax)
www.hayhouse.com® • www.hayfoundation.org

———

Published in Australia by: Hay House Australia Pty. Ltd.,
18/36 Ralph St., Alexandria NSW 2015
Phone: 612-9669-4299 • *Fax:* 612-9669-4144
www.hayhouse.com.au

Published in the United Kingdom by: Hay House UK, Ltd.,
The Sixth Floor, Watson House, 54 Baker Street, London W1U 7BU
Phone: +44 (0)20 3927 7290 • *Fax:* +44 (0)20 3927 7291
www.hayhouse.co.uk

Published in India by: Hay House Publishers India,
Muskaan Complex, Plot No. 3, B-2, Vasant Kunj, New Delhi 110 070
Phone: 91-11-4176-1620 • *Fax:* 91-11-4176-1630
www.hayhouse.co.in

———

Access New Knowledge.
Anytime. Anywhere.

Learn and evolve at your own pace
with the world's leading experts.

www.hayhouseU.com

SOURCES

Page 6: *The Law of Attraction*, Esther and Jerry Hicks
Page 18: *Manifesting Your Magical Life*, Radleigh Valentine
Page 32: *The Power of Intention*, Dr. Wayne W. Dyer
Page 44: *8 Secrets to Powerful Manifesting*, Mandy Morris
Page 68: *Super Attractor*, Gabrielle Bernstein
Page 90: *Thank & Grow Rich*, Pam Grout
Page 98: *The Tapping Solution*, Nick Ortner
Page 120: *Mind to Matter*, Dawson Church

HAY HOUSE
Online Video Courses

Your journey to a better life starts with figuring out which path is best for you. Hay House Online Courses provide guidance in mental and physical health, personal finance, telling your unique story, and so much more!

LEARN HOW TO:

- choose your words and actions wisely so you can tap into life's magic

- clear the energy in yourself and your environments for improved clarity, peace, and joy

- forgive, visualize, and trust in order to create a life of authenticity and abundance

- manifest lifelong health by improving nutrition, reducing stress, improving sleep, and more

- create your own unique angelic communication toolkit to help you to receive clear messages for yourself and others

- use the creative power of the quantum realm to create health and well-being

To find the guide for your journey, visit www.HayHouseU.com.

HAY HOUSE
online learning